Holy Hour of Consolation and Reparation to Jesus Christ in Agony

Holy Hour of Consolation and Reparation to Jesus Christ in Agony

FOR EVERY DAY OF THE WEEK

Rev. Fr. Evaristus Eshiowu FSSP

Nihil Obstat
Very Rev. Fr Joe Frazer
Vicar General
Diocese of Sacramento, CA

Imprimatur
His Excellency
+Most Rev. Jaime Soto
Bishop of Sacramento, CA
February, 2021.

Edited By
Rev. Fr. J. Curtis, FSSP, Pastor
St. Stephen's Catholic Church
Sacramento, CA.

PALMETTO
P U B L I S H I N G
Charleston, SC
www.PalmettoPublishing.com

Copyright © 2024 by Rev. Fr. Evaristus Eshiowu FSSP

All rights reserved

No portion of this book may be reproduced, stored in a retrieval system, or transmitted in any form by any means–electronic, mechanical, photocopy, recording, or other–except for brief quotations in printed reviews, without prior permission of the author.

Paperback ISBN: 9798822959507
eBook ISBN: 9798822959514

PREFACE

In our time, our Blessed Lord Jesus Christ seems to be suffering more from the wounds inflicted upon Him by the members of His Mystical Body, more than those from His enemies. In the past two decades, the Holy Church has had to go through an unprecedented crisis: from the turmoil of sexual abuses to the present virus pandemic. These crises have affected every aspect of the Church's life and ministry. Above all, it has impacted negatively on the faithful.

As the Head of His Mystical Body, the Lord Jesus Christ suffers when the Church is tribulation; a recurrence of His sacred passion. Hence, He asked Peter the Apostle in the garden of Gethsemane: "Can't you watch with me even for one hour?" (Matt. 26:40). This question continues to re-echo in our time. He promptly appreciated the very small favor done to Him by the woman who wiped His bloody face on the way to Calvary. Thus, He will equally appreciate even more, those who will spend time to console Him in the midst of the adversities of His Mystical Body, the Church.

In this composition, we have tried to provide practical meditations on the sufferings of our Lord centered on the Sorrowful Mysteries of the Holy Rosary, for every day of the week. This will help all those who wish to fulfill the request of our Agonizing Lord, to watch with Him even for one hour, whether by day or night. Some families have learnt to assist at Mass, live streamed, from their home because of the pandemic. Similarly, they can adore the Lord from their homes, in reparation for the increasing sins against our Him in the Blessed Sacrament, which is at the center of the crises in the Church.

We pray and hope that the devotion will help to turn the attitude of criticism, anger and frustration of the faithful towards the leaders of the Church, into adoration, consolation and reparation towards the Lord in Agony.

HOW TO MAKE THE HOLY HOUR

This devotion is drawn from what our Lord Jesus Christ called, *His Anguish Appeals,* in one of His private revelations. In the Anguish Appeals, the Lord lamented over a series of sins committed repeatedly against Himself, His Church, the Sacrament of the Most Holy Eucharist and our own selves, in our present generation. Thus, the spirituality of the devotion is based on the theology of the *Mystical Body,* whereby He is the Head of His Church and we are the body. Therefore, any sin committed by or against any member of the Church, renews His Passions which are indicated in His Sorrowful mysteries. *So, the proper disposition for this devotion is that of penance and reparation.*

The ideal place for the devotion is before the Blessed Sacrament, exposed or in the Tabernacle. It can also be done in the home or any other suitable place, with a Cross standing on an altar or hanging on the wall. An altar could be decorated with lighted candles and with flowers, if possible, (except during Lent).

The adoration can be done anytime, but best from 3 am or 3 pm, Hour of Divine Mercy.

The sole intention for the adoration is to *console* our Agonizing Redeemer and make *reparation* for our sins and that of the whole world. Therefore, there is no room for any other private intentions, except as indicated in the *Offering of the merits of the Precious Blood of Jesus (page 11)*.

It can be used by individuals or groups for the regular Holy Hour of Adoration in churches or chapels of perpetual adoration.

Families are encouraged to use it as part of their daily prayers at home. In that case, they should focus their attention towards the Lord Jesus Christ in the tabernacle in their local church, just the same way they were assisting at Mass from their home when the churches were closed during the pandemic.

PILGRIMAGE OF REPARATION

I wish to recommend that individuals and groups of people who feel some special dedication to this devotion, can opt to make *Pilgrimages of Reparation* to different churches in their dioceses, at least once a week, to make reparation for any acts of irreverence, desecration or sacrilege which may have taken place there. They will simply make this Holy Hour of Consolation and Reparation in the Church. This will be in addition to propagating the devotion itself.

Dedicated to:

The Sorrowful Immaculate Heart of Mary

At the Foot of the Cross

CONTENTS

SUNDAY   1

Introduction	3
First Sorrowful Mystery	6
Second Sorrowful Mystery	7
Third Sorrowful Mystery	8
Fourth Sorrowful Mystery	9
Fifth Sorrowful Mystery	10
Conclusion	11
Cross of Grace	12
Litany of the Precious Blood of our Lord Jesus Christ	14
Prayer to Jesus Christ Crucified	17
Offering of the Merits of the Most Precious Blood of our Lord Jesus Christ	19
Act of Reparation to the Most Sacred Heart of Jesus	23

MONDAY   27

Introduction	29
First Sorrowful Mystery	30
Second Sorrowful Mystery	31
Third Sorrowful Mystery	32
Fourth Sorrowful Mystery	33
Fifth Sorrowful Mystery	34

Conclusion 35
Act of Reparation to Jesus in the Most Blessed Sacrament 37

TUESDAY 39

Introduction 41
First Sorrowful Mystery 42
Second Sorrowful Mystery 43
Third Sorrowful Mystery 44
Fourth Sorrowful Mystery 45
Fifth Sorrowful Mystery 46
Conclusion 47
Act of Dedication of Human Race to the Most
Sacred Heart of Jesus. 49

WEDNESDAY 51

Introduction 53
First Sorrowful Mystery 54
Second Sorrowful Mystery 55
Third Sorrowful Mystery 56
Fourth Sorrowful Mystery 57
Fifth Sorrowful Mystery 58
Conclusion 59
Prayer to St. Joseph 60

THURSDAY 63

Introduction	65
First Sorrowful Mystery	66
Second Sorrowful Mystery	67
Third Sorrowful Mystery	68
Fourth Sorrowful Mystery	69
Fifth Sorrowful Mystery	70
Conclusion	71
Prayer to Obtain the Sanctification of the Clergy	72

FRIDAY 75

Introduction	77
First Sorrowful Mystery	78
Second Sorrowful Mystery	79
Third Sorrowful Mystery	80
Fourth Sorrowful Mystery	81
Fifth Sorrowful Mystery	82
Conclusion	83
Prayer to the Crucified Lord Jesus Christ	84

SATURDAY 87

Introduction	89
First Sorrowful Mystery	90

Second Sorrowful Mystery	91
Third Sorrowful Mystery	92
Fourth Sorrowful Mystery	93
Fifth Sorrowful Mystery	94
Conclusion	95
An Act of Reparation for Blasphemies against the Blessed Virgin Mary	97
Prayer to Our Lady of Sorrows	98

SUNDAY

INTRODUCTION

General Intention. Consolation for the Sorrows of our Lord Jesus Christ during His Passion; Reparation for the sins against Holy Mother the Church.

Opening Hymn.

God of Mercy and Compassion.

God of Mercy and Compassion
Look with pity upon me
Father let me call Thee Father,
Bid Thy child return to Thee

Chorus
Jesus Lord, I ask for mercy,
Let me not implore in vain;
All my sins I now detest them,
Never will I sin again.

By my sins, I have deserved,
Death and endless misery;
Hell with its pains and torments,
And for all eternity.

By my sins I have abandoned,
Right and claim to Heaven above;
Where the Saint rejoice forever,
In a boundless sea of love.

See my Savior bleeding dying,
On the Cross of Calvary;
To that Cross my sins have nailed Him,
Yet He bleeds and dies for me.

(Or Any other Lenten Hymn)

Declaration of Intention.

Dearest Agonizing Jesus Christ, I console Thee and adore Thy Most Precious Blood, in reparation for my sins and the sins of the whole world.

V. Come O Holy Ghost and fill the hearts of the faithful.
R. And enkindle in them the fire of Thy Love
V. Send forth Thy Spirit and they shall be created.
R. And Thou shall renew the face of the earth.

Let us pray. O God, Who, by the light of the Holy Spirit didst instruct the heart of the faithful. Grant that by the same Spirit, we may be truly wise and ever rejoice in His holy consolation. Through Christ our Lord. Amen.

Creed. Our Father.
Hail Mary (3x). Glory be.

O my Jesus, forgive us our sins, save us from the fires of hell, lead all souls to Heaven, especially those who are most in need of your mercy.

FIRST SORROWFUL MYSTERY

The Agony in the Garden

Petition. May the Lord grant us the grace of perfect sorrow for our sins and a perfect obedience to His holy will. Amen.

Consolation. Dearest Agonizing Jesus Christ, we console Thee for the Sorrows that filled Thy Heart during Thy Agony in the Garden of Gethsemane, when thinking about the future plight of Thy Holy Church.

Reparation. We make reparation for the sins of the frequent invasion Thy Sanctuaries and desecration of Your Altars in our time.

Atonement Prayer. Calm the heat of Your anger, O Lord. We are sorry, we all have sinned, we will never sin again. St. Michael the Archangel with your light enlighten us, with your wings protect us, and with your sword defend us. Amen.

Our Father. Hail Mary (10x).
Glory be. O my Jesus.

SECOND SORROWFUL MYSTERY
The Scourging at the Pillar

Petition. May the Lord grant us the grace to mortify our senses perfectly. Amen.

Consolation. Dearest Agonizing Jesus Christ, we console Thee for Thy Sorrows during the scourging at the Pilar, whereby Thy Sacred Body was severely lacerated.

Reparation. We make reparation for the frequent acts of irreverence and desecration of the Sacraments in Thy churches during Divine worship.

Atonement Prayer. Calm the heat of Your anger, O Lord. We are sorry, we all have sinned, we will never sin again. St. Michael the Archangel with your light enlighten us, with your wings protect us, and with your sword defend us. Amen.

Our Father. Hail Mary (10x).
Glory be. O my Jesus.

THIRD SORROWFUL MYSTERY
The Crowning with Thorns

Petition. May the Lord grant us the grace of true contempt for the world, its honors and riches. Amen.

Consolation. Dearest Agonizing Jesus Christ, we console Thee for Thy Sorrows during the crowning with Thorns; as Thy Sacred Head was tormented with thorns, while You were insulted with mockery and blasphemies.

Reparation. We make reparation for the sins of doctrinal errors and heresies introduced into the Church by Thine enemies.

Atonement Prayer. Calm the heat of Your anger, O Lord. We are sorry, we all have sinned, we will never sin again. St. Michael the Archangel with your light enlighten us, with your wings protect us, and with your sword defend us. Amen.

> *Our Father. Hail Mary (10x).*
> *Glory be. O my Jesus.*

FOURTH SORROWFUL MYSTERY
The Carrying of the Cross

Petition. May the Lord grant us the grace of patiently carrying our crosses everyday of our lives, in imitation of His footsteps. Amen.

Consolation. Dearest Agonizing Jesus Christ, we console Thee for Thy Sorrows, while carrying the Cross on the way to Calvary. You fell several times full of anguish over the lukewarmness of many of Thy followers.

Reparation. We make reparation for the sins of rejection of the cross and loss of faith among the faithful in the Church.

Atonement Prayer. Calm the heat of Your anger, O Lord. We are sorry, we all have sinned, we will never sin again. St. Michael the Archangel with your light enlighten us, with your wings protect us, and with your sword defend us. Amen.

Our Father. Hail Mary (10x).
Glory be. O my Jesus.

FIFTH SORROWFUL MYSTERY
The Crucifixion & Death of Our Lord

Petition. May the Lord grant us the grace of horror for sin, love of the Cross and holy death for ourselves. May He be merciful to all those in their last agony. Amen.

Consolation. Dearest Agonising Jesus Christ, we console Thee for Thy sorrows while hanging on the Cross, mindful of the crisis that will befall Thy Holy Church through the ages.

Reparation. We make reparation for the sins of those who castigate and blaspheme the Church in the time of her affliction, the neglect and lukewarmness of some of Her leaders.

Atonement Prayer. Calm the heat of Your anger, O Lord. We are sorry, we all have sinned, we will never sin again. St. Michael the Archangel with your light enlighten us, with your wings protect us, and with your sword defend us. Amen.

Our Father. Hail Mary (10x).
Glory be. O my Jesus.

CONCLUSION

Hail Holy Queen, Mother of mercy. Hail our life, our sweetness and our hope. To You do cry, poor banished children of Eve. To You do we raise up heart mourning and weeping in this valley of tears. Turn then, most gracious advocate, Your eyes of mercy towards us. And after this our exile, show unto us the Blessed fruit of Your womb, Jesus. O Clement, O loving, O sweet Virgin Mary.

V. Pray for us O Holy Mother of God.
R. That we may be made worthy of the promises of Christ.

Let us pray. O God, whose only Begotten Son, by His life, death and resurrection, has purchased for us the reward of eternal life. Grant, we beseech Thee, that, meditating upon the mysteries of the most Holy Rosary of the Blessed Virgin Mary, we may imitate what they contain and obtain what they promise, through the same Christ our Lord.

V. Most Sacred Heart of Jesus.
R. Have mercy on us.
V. Immaculate of Mary.
R. Pray for us.
V. St. Joseph, husband of Mary
R. Pray for us.
V. St. John the Evangelist.
R. Pray for us.
V. St. Louis Marie de Montfort.
R. Pray for us.

CROSS OF GRACE

From Montichiari - Fontanelle, Italy

Conscious, merciful Savior, of my nothingness and Thy sublimity, I cast myself at Thy Feet and thank Thee for the many proofs of Thy grace shown to me, Thy ungrateful creature. I thank Thee especially for delivering me by Thy Precious Blood, from the destructive power of Satan.

In the presence of my dear Mother, Mary, my Guardian Angel and patron Saints, and of the whole company of Heaven, I dedicate myself voluntarily with a sincere heart, O dearest Jesus, to Thy Precious Blood, by which Thou hast redeemed the world from sin, death and hell. I promise Thee, with the help of Thy grace and to the utmost of my strength to stir up and foster devotion to Thy Precious Blood, the price of our redemption, so that Thy Adorable Blood may be honored and glorified by all. In this way, I wish to make reparation for my disloyalty towards Thy Precious Blood of love, and to make satisfaction to Thee for the many profanations which men commit against that precious Price of their salvation.

O would that my own sins, my coldness, and the acts of disrespect I have ever committed against Thee, O holy Precious Blood could be undone. Behold, O dearest Jesus, I offer to Thee the love, honor and adoration, which Thy Most Holy Mother, Thy faithful disciples and all the Saints have offered to Thy Precious Blood.

I ask Thee to forget my earlier faithlessness and coldness, and forgive all who offend Thee. Sprinkle me, O Divine Savior, and men with Thy Precious Blood, so that we, O Crucified Love, may love Thee from now on with all our hearts, and worthily honor the Price of our salvation. Amen.

LITANY OF THE PRECIOUS BLOOD OF OUR LORD JESUS CHRIST

V. Lord have mercy on us.
R. Lord have mercy on us.
V. Christ have mercy on us.
R. Christ have mercy on us.
V. Lord have mercy on us, Christ hear us.
R. Christ graciously hear us.
V. God, the Father of Heaven.
R. Have mercy on us.

V. God the Son, Redeemer of the world.
R. Have mercy on us.
V. God the Holy Ghost.
R. Have mercy on us.
V. Holy Trinity, One God.
R. Have mercy on us

Blood of Christ, Only-Begotten of the Father.
Save us.
Blood of Christ, Incarnate Word of God.
Save us.
Blood of Christ, of the New and Eternal Testament.
Save us.
Blood of Christ, falling upon the earth in the Agony.
Save us.
Blood of Christ, shed profusely in the Scourging.
Save us.
Blood of Christ, flowing forth in the Crowning with Thorns.
Save us.
Blood of Christ, poured out on the Cross.
Save us.
Blood of Christ, Price of our salvation.
Save us.

Blood of Christ, without which there will be no forgiveness.

Save us.

Blood of Christ, Eucharistic Drink and refreshment of souls.

Save us.

Blood of Christ, Stream of Mercy.

Save us.

Blood of Christ, Victor over demons.

Save us.

Blood of Christ, Courage of Martyrs.

Save us.

Blood of Christ, Strength of Confessors.

Save us.

Blood of Christ, bringing forth Virgins.

Save us.

Blood of Christ, Help of those in peril.

Save us.

Blood of Christ, Relief of the burdened.

Save us.

Blood of Christ, Solace in sorrow.

Save us.

Blood of Christ, Hope of the penitent.

Save us.

Blood of Christ, Consolation of the dying.
Save us.
Blood of Christ, Peace and tenderness of hearts.
Save us.
Blood of Christ, Pledge of Eternal life.
Save us.
Blood of Christ, freeing souls from purgatory.
Save us.
Blood of Christ, Most worthy of all Glory and Honor.
Save us.
Lamb of God Who takes away the sins of the world.
Spare us, O Lord.
Lamb of God, Who takes away the sins of the world.
Graciously hear us, O Lord.
Lamb of God, Who takes away the sins of the world.
Have mercy on us.

V. Thou hast redeemed us, O Lord, in Thy Blood.
R. And made us for our God, a Kingdom.

Let us pray. Almighty and ever-lasting God, Who didst appoint Thine Only-Begotten Son, the Redeemer of the world, and hast willed to be appeased by His Blood; grant, we beseech Thee, so to venerate with solemn worship, the Price of our redemption, and by Its power be defended against the evils of this life; that we may enjoy the fruit thereof forevermore, in heaven. Through the same Lord Jesus Christ Thy Son, Who liveth and reigneth with Thee; in the unity of Holy Ghost, God world without end. Amen.

PRAYER TO JESUS CHRIST CRUCIFIED

O God, Who for the redemption of the world, didst will to be born amongst men, to be circumcised, to be rejected by the Jews, to be betrayed by the traitor Judas with a kiss, to be bound with cords, to be led to the slaughter as an innocent Lamb, to be shamelessly exposed to the gaze of Annas, Caiaphas, Pilate and Herod; to be accused by false witnesses, to be tormented by scourges and insults, defiled with spitting, crowned with thorns, smitten with blows, struck with a reed, blindfolded, stripped of Thy garments, fastened to the Cross, reckoned among thieves, given gall and vinegar to drink and wounded with a spear.

Do Thou, O Lord, by these Thy most Holy Sufferings, upon which I unworthily meditate; and by Thy Holy Cross and death, deliver me from the pains of hell, and vouchsafe to bring me where Thou didst bring the repentant thief who was crucified with Thee, Who with the Father and the Holy Ghost lives and reigns, one God, world without end. Amen.

Our Father. Hail Mary. Glory be (3x).

Prayer

Lord Jesus Christ, Who comes down from Heaven to the earth from the Bosom of the Father, and didst shed Thy Precious Blood for the remission of our sins: we humbly beseech Thee, that in the day of judgment, we may deserve to hear, standing at Thy Right Hand: "Come, ye blessed." Who lives and reigns forever and ever. Amen.

OFFERING OF THE MERITS OF THE MOST PRECIOUS BLOOD OF OUR LORD JESUS CHRIST

1. **Eternal Father**, I offer Thee the merits of the Precious Blood of Jesus, Thy beloved Son, my Savior and my God, for the spread and exaltation of our dear Mother, Thy Holy Church, for the preservation and welfare of Her visible Head, the Sovereign Pontiff, for the Cardinals, Bishops and Pastors of souls, and for all the ministers of the sanctuary.
Glory be to the Father, and to the Son, and to the Holy Ghost; as it was in the beginning is now and ever shall be, world without end. Amen.

V. Blessed and praised forever more be Jesus.
R. Who hath saved us with His Blood.

2. **Eternal Father,** I offer Thee the merit of the Precious Blood of Jesus, Thy Beloved Son, my Savior and my God, for peace and concord among Christian political leaders, for the humbling of the enemies of our Holy Faith and for the welfare of all Thy Christian people.
Glory be.

V. Blessed and praised forever more be Jesus.
R. Who hath saved us with His Blood.

3. **Eternal Father,** I offer Thee, the merits of the Precious Blood of Jesus, Thy beloved Son, my Savior and my God, for the conversion of unbelievers, the rooting up of all heresies and the conversion of sinners.
Glory be.

V. Blessed and praised forever more be Jesus.
R. Who hath saved us with His Blood.

4. **Eternal Father,** I offer Thee the merits of the Precious Blood of Jesus, Thy beloved Son, my Savior and my God, for all my relations, benefactors, friends and enemies,; for those in need, in sickness and tribulation, and all those for whom Thou knowest that I am bound to pray, and will that I should pray.
Glory be.

V. Blessed and praised forever more be Jesus.
R. Who hath saved us with His Blood.

5. **Eternal Father,** I offer Thee the merits of the Precious Blood of Jesus, Thy beloved Son, my Savior and my God, for all those who are to pass this day to the other life, deliver them from the pains of hell, and admit them with all speed to the possession of Thy Glory.
Glory be.

V. Blessed and praised forever more be Jesus.
R. Who hath saved us with His Blood.

6. **Eternal Father,** I offer Thee the merits of the Precious Blood of Jesus, Thy beloved Son, my Savior and my God, for all men who are lovers of this great treasure and who are intended with me in adoring and glorifying It, and labor to spread this devotion.
Glory be.

V. Blessed and praised forever more be Jesus.
R. Who hath saved us with His Blood.

7. **Eternal Father,** I offer Thee the merits of the Precious Blood of Jesus, Thy beloved Son, my Savior and my God, for all my needs, both

temporal and spiritual, as an intercession for the holy souls in Purgatory, and in a special manner for those who were most devoted to this price of our Redemption and to the sorrows and suffering of our dear Mother, Mary most Holy.
Glory be.

V. Blessed and praised forever more be Jesus.
R. Who hath saved us with His Blood.

Glory be to the Blood of Jesus both now and for evermore and through everlasting ages. Amen.

Prayer

Almighty and everlasting God, Who hast appointed Thine only Begotten Son to be the Redeemer of the world, and hast been pleased to be reconciled unto us by His Blood. Grant us, we beseech Thee, so to venerate with solemn worship the price of our salvation, that the power thereof may here on earth, keep us from all things hurtful, and the fruits of the same may gladden us forever hereafter in Heaven. Through the same Christ our Lord. Amen.

ACT OF REPARATION TO THE MOST SACRED HEART OF JESUS

From Holy Hour of Reparation to the Sacred Heart of Jesus – Soul Assurance

O Sacred Heart of Jesus, animated with a desire to repair the unceasing outrages offered to Thee, we prostrate before Thy Throne of mercy, and in the name of all mankind, pledge our love and fidelity to Thee.

The more Thy mysteries are blasphemed, the more firmly we shall believe them, O Sacred Heart of Jesus.

The more impiety endeavors to extinguish our hopes of immortality, the more we shall trust in Thy Heart, sole hope of mankind.

The more hearts resist Thy Divine attractions, the more we shall love Thee, O infinitely amiable Heart of Jesus.

The more unbelief attacks Thy Divinity, the more humbly and profoundly we shall adore It, O Divine Heart of Jesus.

The more Thy holy laws are transgressed and ignored, the more we shall delight to observe them, O most Holy Heart of Jesus.

The more Thy Sacraments are despised and abandoned, the more frequently we shall receive them with love and reverence, O most liberal Heart of Jesus.

The more the imitation of Thy virtues are neglected and forgotten, the more we shall endeavor to practice them, O Heart, model of all virtues.

The more the devil labors to destroy souls, the more we shall be inflamed with the desire to save them, O Heart of Jesus, zealous Lover of souls.

The more sin and impurity destroy the image of God in man, the more we shall try by purity of life, to be living temples of the Holy Spirit, O Heart of Jesus.

The more Thy Holy Church is despised, the more we shall endeavor to be her faithful children, O sweet Heart of Jesus.

The more Thy Vicar on earth is persecuted, the more will we honor him as the infallible head of Thy Holy Church, show our fidelity and pray for him, O Kingly Heart of Jesus.

O Sacred Heart, through Thy powerful grace, may we become Thine apostles in the midst of a corrupted world, and be Thy crown in the Kingdom of Heaven. Amen.

Prayer to the Blessed Virgin Mary

We fly to Thy patronage, O Holy Mother of God; despise not our prayers, in our necessities, but deliver from all dangers, O ever glorious and Blessed Virgin Mary. Amen.

MONDAY

INTRODUCTION

General Intention. Consolation for the pains of our Lord Jesus Christ during His Passion and, Reparation for the sins against the Sacrament of the Most Holy Eucharist.

Opening Hymn. God of Mercy. (*as on page 4, or any Lenten Hymn*)

Declaration of Intention. Dearest Agonizing Jesus Christ, I console Thee and adore Thy Most Precious Blood, in reparation for my sins and the sins of the whole world.

V. Come O Holy Ghost and fill the hearts of the faithful.
R. And enkindle in them the fire of Thy Love
V. Send forth Thy Spirit and they shall be created.
R. And Thou shall renew the face of the earth.

Let us pray. O God, Who, by the light of the Holy Ghost didst instruct the heart of the faithful. Grant that by the same Spirit, we may be truly wise and ever rejoice in His holy consolation. Through Christ our Lord. Amen.

Creed. Our Father. Hail Mary (x3).
Glory be.

O my Jesus, forgive us our sins, save us from the fires of hell, lead all souls to Heaven, especially those who are most in need of Your mercy.

FIRST SORROWFUL MYSTERY
The Agony in the Garden

Petition. May the Lord grant us the grace of perfect sorrow for our sins and a perfect obedience to His holy will. Amen.

Consolation. Dearest Agonizing Jesus Christ, we console Thee for all the pains Thou endured during the night of Thy incarceration by the cruel soldiers before the trial in the court of Pontus Pilate.

Reparation. We make reparation for the outrageous desecrations of the Most Blessed Sacrament in our churches.

Atonement Prayer. Jesus in the Holy Eucharist, we are sorry, for all the sins committed against Thee on earth. St. Michael the Archangel with your light enlighten us, with your wings protect us, and with your sword defend us. Amen.

Our Father. Hail Mary (10x).
Glory be. O my Jesus.

SECOND SORROWFUL MYSTERY
The Scourging at the Pillar

Petition. May the Lord grant us the grace to mortify our senses perfectly. Amen.

Consolation. Dearest Agonizing Jesus Christ, we console You for the pains You endured during Your scourging at the Pillar; on the Sacred Body which You offered in Sacrifice during the Last Supper for our redemption.

Reparation. We make reparation for the sins of Sacrilege against the Most Holy Eucharist by those who receive or administer It unworthily.

Atonement Prayer. Jesus in the Holy Eucharist, we are sorry, for all the sins committed against Thee on earth. St. Michael the Archangel with your light enlighten us, with your wings protect us, and with your sword defend us. Amen.

Our Father. Hail Mary (10x).
Glory be. O my Jesus.

THIRD SORROWFUL MYSTERY
The Crowning with Thorns

Petition. May the Lord grant us the grace of true contempt for the world, its honors and riches. Amen.

Consolation. Dearest Agonizing Jesus Christ, we console You for the pains You endured when Thy Sacred Head was crowned with thorns and struck with a reed to drive the spikes deep into Thy Sacred brain.

Reparation. We make reparation for the sins of disrespect towards Thy real Presence in the Blessed Sacrament, and Its neglect in churches where It is neither reverenced nor adored.

Atonement Prayer. Jesus in the Holy Eucharist, we are sorry, for all the sins committed against You on earth. St. Michael the Archangel with your light enlighten us, with your wings protect us, and with your sword defend us. Amen.

Our Father. Hail Mary (10x).
Glory be. O my Jesus.

FOURTH SORROWFUL MYSTERY
The Carrying of the Cross

Petition. May the Lord grant us the grace of patiently carrying our crosses everyday of our lives, in imitation of His footsteps. Amen.

Consolation. Dearest Agonizing Jesus Christ, we Console Thee for the pains Thou endured on the way to Calvary, from the wounds on Your Sacred Body, Head and Shoulder; and on Your Knees from frequent falls.

Reparation. We make reparation for the sacrileges of those who receive the Most Blessed Sacrament and take It away for desecration through occultic practices and other evil ways.

Atonement Prayer. Jesus in the Holy Eucharist, we are sorry, for all the sins committed against You on earth. St. Michael the Archangel with your light enlighten us, with your wings protect us, and with your sword defend us. Amen.

Our Father. Hail Mary (10x).
Glory be. O my Jesus.

FIFTH SORROWFUL MYSTERY
The Crucifixion & Death of Our Lord

Petition. May the Lord grant us the grace of horror for sin, love of the Cross and holy death for ourselves. May He be merciful to all those in their last agony. Amen.

Consolation. Dearest Agonizing Jesus Christ, we console Thee for the pains Thou endured on Calvary, from Thy Hands and Feet nailed to the Cross, and Thy Side pierced with a lance.

Reparation. We make reparation for the sins of those who do not receive Holy Communion out of indifference, or as a result of attachment to some habitual sins.

Atonement Prayer. Jesus in the Holy Eucharist, we are sorry, for all the sins committed against You on earth. St. Michael the Archangel with your light enlighten us, with your wings protect us, and with your sword defend us. Amen.

***Our Father. Hail Mary (10x).
Glory be. O my Jesus.***

CONCLUSION

Hail Holy Queen, Mother of mercy. Hail our life, our sweetness and our hope. To Thee do cry, poor banished children of Eve. To Thee do we raise up heart mourning and weeping in this valley of tears. Turn then, most gracious advocate, Thine eyes of mercy towards us. And after this our exile, show unto us the Blessed fruit of Thy womb, Jesus. O Clement, O loving, O sweet Virgin Mary.

V. Pray for us O Holy Mother of God.
R. That we may be made worthy of the promises of Christ.

Let us pray. O God, whose only Begotten Son, by His life, death and resurrection, has purchased for us the reward of eternal life. Grant, we beseech Thee, that, meditating upon the mysteries of the most Holy Rosary of the Blessed Virgin Mary, we may imitate what they contain and obtain what they promise, through the same Christ our Lord.

V. Most Sacred Heart of Jesus.
R. Have mercy on us.
V. Immaculate of Mary.
R. Pray for us.
V. St. Joseph.
R. Pray for us.
V. St. John the Evangelist.
R. Pray for us.
V. St. Louis Maria de Montfort.
R. Pray for us.

ACT OF REPARATION TO JESUS IN THE MOST BLESSED SACRAMENT

With that profound humility which the Faith itself inspires in me, O my God and Savior Jesus Christ, true God and true Man, I love Thee with all my heart, and I adore Thee who art hidden here [in the Blessed Sacrament], in reparation for all the irreverences, profanations and sacrileges which Thou receives in the most Adorable Sacrament of the Altar.

I adore Thee, O my God, if not as much as Thou are worthy to be adored, or so much as I am bound to do, yet as much as I am able. Would that I could adore Thee with that perfect worship which the Angels in Heaven are enabled to offer Thee. May Thou, O my Jesus, be known, adored, loved and thanked by all men at every moment in this most Holy and Divine Sacrament. Amen.

*Continue from page 8, **(Cross of Grace).***

TUESDAY

INTRODUCTION

General Intention. Consolation for the Trial of our Lord Jesus Christ before Caiaphas, Pilate and Herod. Reparation for the sins of betrayal by Religious leaders, Oppression and injustice by secular rulers.

Opening Hymn.
God of Mercy. (*as on page 4, or any Lenten Hymn*)

Declaration of Intention. Dearest Agonizing Jesus Christ, I console Thee and adore Thy Most Precious Blood, in reparation for my sins and the sins of the whole world.

V. Come O Holy Ghost and fill the hearts of the faithful.
R. And enkindle in them the fire of Thy Love
V. Send forth Thy Spirit and they shall be created.
R. And Thou shall renew the face of the earth.

Let us pray. O God, Who, by the light of the Holy Spirit didst instruct the heart of the faithful. Grant that by the same Spirit, we may be truly wise and ever rejoice in His holy consolation. Through Christ our Lord. Amen.

***Creed. Our Father. Hail Mary (x3).
Glory be.***

O my Jesus, forgive us our sins, save us from the fires of hell, lead all souls to Heaven, especially those who are most in need of your mercy.

FIRST SORROWFUL MYSTERY
The Agony in the Garden

Petition. May the Lord grant us the grace of perfect sorrow for our sins and a perfect obedience to His holy will. Amen.

Consolation. Dearest Agonizing Jesus Christ, we console Thee for Thy trial before Caiaphas the High priest, for all the false accusations and testimonies against Thee.

Reparation. We make reparation for the sins of weakness and infidelity by some Religious leaders in Thy Church.

Atonement Prayer. May Your Kingdom reign everywhere on earth, as in Heaven, before the just and the unjust who know You not. St. Michael the Archangel with your light enlighten us, with your wings protect us, and with your sword defend us. Amen.

Our Father. Hail Mary (10x).
Glory be. O my Jesus.

SECOND SORROWFUL MYSTERY
The Scourging at the Pillar

Petition. May the Lord grant us the grace to mortify our senses perfectly. Amen.

Consolation. Dearest Agonizing Jesus Christ, we console Thee for Thy first trial before Pontus Pilate who publicly declared Thee innocent of any crime, and yet refused to set Thee free.

Reparation. We make reparation for the sins of suppression of the Truth and promotion of falsehood among world rulers.

Atonement Prayer. May Thy Kingdom reign everywhere on earth, as in Heaven, before the just and the unjust who know Thee not. St. Michael the Archangel with your light enlighten us, with your wings protect us, and with your sword defend us. Amen.

Our Father. Hail Mary (10x).
Glory be. O my Jesus.

THIRD SORROWFUL MYSTERY
The Crowning with Thorns

Petition. May the Lord grant us the grace of true contempt for the world, its honors and riches. Amen.

Consolation. Dearest Agonizing Jesus Christ, we console Thee for the insult of bringing Thee before Herod for trial, who himself was an adulterer and a murderer.

Reparation. We make reparation for the sin of hypocrisy among world rulers and the oppression of the poor and weak.

Atonement Prayer. May Thy Kingdom reign everywhere on earth, as in Heaven, before the just and the unjust who know Thee not. St. Michael the Archangel with your light enlighten us, with your wings protect us, and with your sword defend us. Amen.

Our Father. Hail Mary (10x).
Glory be. O my Jesus.

FOURTH SORROWFUL MYSTERY
The Carrying of the Cross

Petition. May the Lord grant us the grace of patiently carrying our crosses everyday of our lives, in imitation of His footsteps. Amen.

Consolation. Dearest Agonizing Jesus Christ, we console Thee for Thy second appearance before Pilate, at which he released the criminal Barabbas and ordered Thee to be scourged.

Reparation. We make reparation for the deceits of those men and women who obtained political powers, but use them to make laws that violate the rights to life, freedom, and conscience of those who elected them.

Atonement Prayer. May Your Kingdom reign everywhere on earth, as in Heaven, before the just and the unjust who know Thee not. St. Michael the Archangel with your light enlighten us, with your wings protect us, and with your sword defend us. Amen.

Our Father. Hail Mary (10x).
Glory be. O my Jesus.

FIFTH SORROWFUL MYSTERY
The Crucifixion & Death of Our Lord

Petition. May the Lord grant us the grace of horror for sin, love of the Cross and holy death for ourselves. May He be merciful to all those in their last agony. Amen.

Consolation. Dearest Agonizing Jesus Christ, we console Thee for Thy third appearance before Pilate, when he finally condemned Thee to be Crucified.

Reparation. We make reparation for those in the judiciary who deliver judgments for political and personal gains.

Atonement Prayer. May Thy Kingdom reign everywhere on earth, as in Heaven, before the just and the unjust who know Thee not. St. Michael the Archangel with your light enlighten us, with your wings protect us, and with your sword defend us. Amen.

Our Father. Hail Mary (10x).
Glory be. O my Jesus.

CONCLUSION

Hail Holy Queen, Mother of mercy. Hail our life, our sweetness and our hope. To Thee do cry, poor banished children of Eve. To Thee do we raise up heart mourning and weeping in this valley of tears. Turn then, most gracious advocate, Thine eyes of mercy towards us. And after this our exile, show unto us the Blessed fruit of Thy womb, Jesus. O Clement, O loving, O sweet Virgin Mary.

V. Pray for us O Holy Mother of God.
R. That we may be made worthy of the promises of Christ.

Let us pray. O God, whose only Begotten Son, by His life, death and resurrection, has purchased for us the reward of eternal life. Grant, we beseech Thee, that, meditating upon the mysteries of the most Holy Rosary of the Blessed Virgin Mary, we may imitate what they contain and obtain what they promise, through the same Christ our Lord.

V. Most Sacred Heart of Jesus.
R. Have mercy on us.
V. Immaculate of Mary.
R. Pray for us.
V. St. Joseph.
R. Pray for us.
V. St. John the Evangelist.
R. Pray for us.
V. St. Louis Maria de Montfort.
R. Pray for us.

ACT OF DEDICATION OF HUMAN RACE TO THE MOST SACRED HEART OF JESUS.

My most sweet Jesus, Redeemer of the human race, look down upon us humbly prostrate before Thine Divine Presence *(or Thine Altar, if in the church)*. We are Thine, and Thine we wish to be; but to be more surely united with Thee, behold each one of us freely consecrates himself today to Thy most Sacred Heart.

Many, indeed, have never known Thee; many, too, despising Thy precepts have rejected Thee. Have mercy on them all, most merciful Jesus, and draw them to Thy Sacred Heart.

Be Thou King, O Lord, not only of the faithful who have never forsaken Thee, but also of the prodigal children who have abandoned Thee; grant that they may quickly return to their Father's house, lest they die of wretched-ness and hunger.

Be Thou King of those who are deceived by erroneous opinions, or whom discord keeps aloof, and call them back to the harbor of Truth and unity of faith, so that soon there may be one flock and one Shepherd.

Grant O Lord, to Thy Church assurance of freedom and immunity from harm; give peace and order to all nations, and make the earth resound from pole to pole with one cry: Praise to the Divine Heart that wrought our salvation; to It be honor and glory forever. Amen.

*Continue prayers from page 8, **Cross of Grace**.*

WEDNESDAY

INTRODUCTION

General Intention. Consolation for the blasphemies and mockeries of our Lord Jesus Christ during His Passion, and reparation for the sins of the flesh that desecrate the body, and degrade of the family.

Opening Hymn.
God of Mercy. (*as on page 4, or any Lenten Hymn*)

Declaration of Intention. Dearest Agonizing Jesus Christ, I console Thee and adore Your Most Precious Blood, in reparation for my sins and the sins of the whole world.

V. Come O Holy Ghost and fill the hearts of the faithful.
R. And enkindle in them the fire of Thy Love
V. Send forth Thy Spirit and they shall be created.
R. And Thou shall renew the face of the earth.

Let us pray. O God, Who, by the light of the Holy Spirit didst instruct the heart of the faithful. Grant that by the same Spirit, we may be truly wise and ever rejoice in His holy consolation. Through Christ our Lord. Amen.

*Creed. Our Father. Hail Mary (x3).
Glory be.*

O my Jesus, forgive us our sins, save us from the fires of hell, lead all souls to Heaven, especially those who are most in need of your mercy.

FIRST SORROWFUL MYSTERY
The Agony in the Garden

Petition. May the Lord grant us the grace of perfect sorrow for our sins and a perfect obedience to His holy will. Amen.

Consolation. Dearest Agonizing Jesus Christ, we console Thee for the insults and derision Thou received during Thy trial before Caiaphas the High Priest and his council.

Reparation. We make reparation for the sins of contraception, sterilization and other forms of birth control that violate the commandments of God.

Atonement Prayer. Jesus in the Holy Eucharist, may we stop sinning to bring You joy, and bring peace to ourselves in life. St. Michael the Archangel with your light enlighten us, with your wings protect us, and with your sword defend us. Amen.

Our Father. Hail Mary (10x).
Glory be. O my Jesus.

SECOND SORROWFUL MYSTERY
The Scourging at the Pillar

Petition. May the Lord grant us the grace to mortify our senses perfectly. Amen.

Consolation. Dearest Agonizing Jesus Christ, we console Thee for the outrageous blasphemies and insults uttered against Thee during Your scourging at the pillar.

Reparation. We make reparation for the sins of adultery, fornication, and other sins that desecrate the body and desecrate the family.

Atonement Prayer. Jesus in the Holy Eucharist, may we stop sinning to bring You joy, and bring peace to ourselves in life. St. Michael the Archangel with your light enlighten us, with your wings protect us, and with your sword defend us. Amen.

Our Father. Hail Mary (10 ×).
Glory be. O my Jesus.

THIRD SORROWFUL MYSTERY
The Crowning with Thorns

Petition. May the Lord grant us the grace of true contempt for the world, its honors and riches. Amen.

Consolation. Dearest Agonizing Jesus Christ, we console Thee for the mockery, blasphemy and insults by the soldiers, when they crowned Your Sacred Head with thorns.

Reparation. We make reparation for the depravity of all deviant sins against holy purity and of gender disorientation.

Atonement Prayer. Jesus in the Holy Eucharist, may we stop sinning to bring You joy, and bring peace to ourselves in life. St. Michael the Archangel with your light enlighten us, with your wings protect us, and with your sword defend us. Amen.

Our Father. Hail Mary (10x).
Glory be. O my Jesus.

FOURTH SORROWFUL MYSTERY
The Carrying of the Cross

Petition. May the Lord grant us the grace of patiently carrying our crosses everyday of our lives, in imitation of His footsteps. Amen.

Consolation. Dearest Agonizing Jesus Christ, we console Thee for the heavy Cross Thou carried to Calvary, Thy frequent falls on the way and the taunting and insults of people in the crowd.

Reparation. We make reparation for the sins of immodesty in dress, prostitution, and pornography, which are ravaging the youth and devastating families.

Atonement Prayer. Jesus in the Holy Eucharist, may we stop sinning to bring You joy, and bring peace to ourselves in life. St. Michael the Archangel with your light enlighten us, with your wings protect us, and with your sword defend us. Amen.

Our Father. Hail Mary (10x).
Glory be. O my Jesus.

FIFTH SORROWFUL MYSTERY
The Crucifixion & Death of Our Lord

Petition. May the Lord grant us the grace of horror for sin, love of the Cross and holy death for ourselves. May He be merciful to all those in their last agony. Amen.

Consolation. Dearest Agonizing Jesus Christ, we console Thee for the blasphemy and disparaging insults of the bystanders, and the thief while You were hanging on the Cross.

Reparation. We make reparation for the sins of divorce and remarriage which are destroying the very foundation of sacred marriage and family life.

Atonement Prayer. Jesus in the Holy Eucharist, may we stop sinning to bring You joy, and bring peace to ourselves in life. St. Michael the Archangel with your light enlighten us, with your wings protect us, and with your sword defend us. Amen.

Our Father. Hail Mary (10x).
Glory be. O my Jesus.

CONCLUSION

Hail Holy Queen, Mother of mercy. Hail our life, our sweetness and our hope. To You do we cry, poor banished children of Eve. To You do we raise up heart mourning and weeping in this valley of tears. Turn then, most gracious advocate, Your eyes of mercy towards us. And after this our exile, show unto us the Blessed fruit of Thy womb, Jesus. O Clement, O loving, O sweet Virgin Mary.

V. Pray for us O Holy Mother of God.
R. That we may be made worthy of the promises of Christ.

Let us pray. O God, whose only Begotten Son, by His life, death and resurrection, has purchased for us the reward of eternal life. Grant, we beseech Thee, that, meditating upon the mysteries of the most Holy Rosary of the Blessed Virgin Mary, we may imitate what they contain and obtain what they promise, through the same Christ our Lord.

V. Most Sacred Heart of Jesus.
R. Have mercy on us.
V. Immaculate of Mary.
R. Pray for us.
V. St. Joseph.
R. Pray for us.
V. St. John the Evangelist.
R. Pray for us.
V. St. Louis Maria de Montfort.
R. Pray for us.

PRAYER TO ST. JOSEPH

To You, O blessed St. Joseph, we have recourse in our tribulation, and having implored the help of Your thrice-holy Spouse, we confidently invoke Your patronage also. By that charity wherewith You were united to the Immaculate Virgin Mother of God, and by that fatherly affection with which You embraced the Child Jesus, we beseech You, and we humbly pray, that You look graciously upon the inheritance which Jesus Christ has purchased by His Blood, and assist us in our needs by your power and strength.

Most watchful guardian of the Holy Family, protect the chosen people of Jesus Christ; keep far from us all blight of error and corruption: mercifully assist us from Heaven, most mighty defender, in this our conflict with the powers of darkness; and, even as of old, You did rescue the Child Jesus from the supreme peril to His life, so now defend God's Holy Church from the snares of the enemy and from all adversity; keep us one and all under thy continual protection, that we may be supported by your example and thy assistance, may be enabled to lead a holy life and die a happy death and come at last to the possession of everlasting blessedness in Heaven. Amen.

Continue prayers from page 8, ***Cross of Grace***.

THURSDAY

INTRODUCTION

General Intention. Consolation for the Sacred Wounds of our Lord Jesus Christ and reparation for the sins of the clergy and religious.

Opening Hymn. God of Mercy. (*as on page 4, or any Lenten Hymn*)

Declaration of Intention. Dearest Agonizing Jesus Christ, I console Thee and adore Thy Most Precious Blood, in reparation for my sins and the sins of the whole world.

- **V.** Come O Holy Ghost and fill the hearts of the faithful.
- **R.** And enkindle in them the fire of Thy Love
- **V.** Send forth Thy Spirit and they shall be created.
- **R.** And Thou shall renew the face of the earth.

Let us pray. O God, Who, by the light of the Holy Spirit didst instruct the heart of the faithful. Grant that by the same Spirit, we may be truly wise and ever rejoice in His holy consolation. Through Christ our Lord. Amen.

Creed. Our Father. Hail Mary (3×). Glory be.

O my Jesus, forgive us our sins, save us from the fires of hell, lead all souls to Heaven, especially those who are most in need of your mercy.

FIRST SORROWFUL MYSTERY
The Agony in the Garden

Petition. May the Lord grant us the grace of perfect sorrow for our sins and a perfect obedience to His holy will. Amen.

Consolation. Dearest Agonizing Jesus Christ, we console Thee for all the wounds inflicted on Thy Sacred Body during Thy secret tortures.

Reparation. We make reparation for the sins of those who entered the priesthood with the hidden intention to defame the Church.

Atonement Prayer. Jesus in the Holy Eucharist, when You called us, we knew nothing, forgive us we pray Thee Lord, St. Michael the Archangel with your light enlighten us, with your wings protect us, and with your sword defend us. Amen.

Our Father. Hail Mary (10×).
Glory be. O my Jesus.

SECOND SORROWFUL MYSTERY
The Scourging at the Pillar

Petition. May the Lord grant us the grace to mortify our senses perfectly. Amen.

Consolation. Dearest Agonizing Jesus Christ, we console You for the numerous wounds inflicted on Thy Sacred Body during Thy scourging at the pillar.

Reparation. We make reparation for the sins of the clergy against their sacred vow of celibacy, and the scandal of sexual abuse.

Atonement Prayer. Jesus in the Holy Eucharist, when You called us, we knew nothing, forgive us we pray Thee Lord, St. Michael the Archangel with your light enlighten us, with your wings protect us, and with your sword defend us. Amen.

Our Father. Hail Mary (10×).
Glory be. O my Jesus.

THIRD SORROWFUL MYSTERY
The Crowning with Thorns

Petition. May the Lord grant us the grace of true contempt for the world, its honors and riches. Amen.

Consolation. Dearest Agonizing Jesus Christ, we console Thee for the multiple wounds inflicted on Thy Sacred Head during Your painful crowning with thorns.

Reparation. We make reparation for the sins of disobedience and inordinate quest for worldly honors and riches among some members of the clergy.

Atonement Prayer. Jesus in the Holy Eucharist, when You called us, we knew nothing , forgive us we pray Thee, Lord. St. Michael the Archangel with your light enlighten us, with your wings protect us, and with your sword defend us. Amen.

Our Father. Hail Mary. (10×)
Glory be. O my Jesus.

FOURTH SORROWFUL MYSTERY
The Carrying of the Cross

Petition. May the Lord grant us the grace of patiently carrying our crosses everyday of our lives, in imitation of His footsteps. Amen.

Consolation. Dearest Agonizing Jesus Christ, we console Thee for the wounds Thou received on Thy Sacred Shoulder, and on Your Knees when You fell several times on the way to Calvary.

Reparation. We make reparation for the sins of religious men and women against their sacred vows of chastity, poverty and obedience.

Atonement Prayer. Jesus in the Holy Eucharist, when You called us, we knew nothing, forgive us we pray Thee Lord. St. Michael the Archangel with your light enlighten us, with your wings protect us, and with your sword defend us. Amen.

***Our Father. Hail Mary (10×).
Glory be. O my Jesus.***

FIFTH SORROWFUL MYSTERY
The Crucifixion & Death of Our Lord

Petition. May the Lord grant us the grace of horror for sin, love of the Cross and holy death for ourselves. May He be merciful to all those in their last agony. Amen.

Consolation. Dearest Agonizing Jesus Christ, we console You for the five Most Precious Wounds on Your Hands, Feet and Side during Your crucifixion.

Reparation. We make reparation for the sins of sacrilege by members of the clergy who celebrate the Sacraments unworthily, and those who left the clerical state or religious life because of public scandal.

Atonement Prayer. Jesus in the Holy Eucharist, when You called us, we knew nothing, for give us we pray Thee Lord. St. Michael the Archangel with your light enlighten us, with your wings protect us, and with your sword defend us. Amen.

Our Father. Hail Mary (10×).
Glory be. O my Jesus.

CONCLUSION

Hail Holy Queen, Mother of mercy. Hail our life, our sweetness and our hope. To You do we cry, poor banished children of Eve. To You do we raise up heart mourning and weeping in this valley of tears. Turn then, most gracious advocate, Your eyes of mercy towards us. And after this our exile, show unto us the Blessed fruit of Thy womb, Jesus. O Clement, O loving, O sweet Virgin Mary.

V. Pray for us O Holy Mother of God.
R. That we may be made worthy of the promises of Christ.

Let us pray. O God, whose only Begotten Son, by His life, death and resurrection, has purchased for us the reward of eternal life. Grant, we beseech Thee, that, meditating upon the mysteries of the most Holy Rosary of the Blessed Virgin Mary, we may imitate what they contain and obtain what they promise, through the same Christ our Lord.

V. Most Sacred Heart of Jesus.
R. Have mercy on us.
V. Immaculate of Mary.
R. Pray for us.
V. St. Joseph.
R. Pray for us.
V. St. John the Evangelist.
R. Pray for us.
V. St. Louis Maria de Montfort.
R. Pray for us.

PRAYER TO OBTAIN THE SANCTIFICATION OF THE CLERGY

O Jesus, Eternal High Priest, divine Sacrificer, Thou who in an unspeakable burst of love for men, Thy brethren, didst cause the Christian priesthood to spring forth from Thy Sacred Heart, vouchsafe to pour forth upon Thy priests continual living streams of infinite love.

Live in them, transform them into Thee; make them, by Thy grace, fit instruments of Thy mercy; do Thou act in them and through them, and grant that they may become wholly one with Thee by their faithful imitation of Thy virtues; and in Thy name and by the strength of Thy Spirit, may they do the works which Thou didst accomplish for the salvation of the world.

Divine Redeemer of souls, behold how great is the multitude of those who still sleep in the darkness of error; reckon up the number of those Thy unfaithful sheep who stray to the edge of the precipice; console the throngs of the poor, the hungry, ignorant and the feeble who groan in their abandoned condition.

Return to us in the person of Thy priests, truly live again in them; act through them and pass once more through the world, teaching, forgiving, comforting, sacrificing and renewing the sacred bonds of love between the Heart of God and the heart of man. Amen.

Continue prayers from page 8, ***Cross of Grace****.*

FRIDAY

INTRODUCTION

General Intention. Adoration for the Most Precious Blood of Jesus Christ shed during His Passion. Reparation for the crime of shedding of innocent blood.

Opening Hymn. God of Mercy. (*as on page 4, or any Lenten Hymn*)

Declaration of Intention. Dearest Agonizing Jesus Christ, I console Thee and adore Thy Most Precious Blood, in reparation for my sins and the sins of the whole world.

V. Come O Holy Ghost and fill the hearts of the faithful.
R. And enkindle in them the fire of Thy Love
V. Send forth Thy Spirit and they shall be created.
R. And Thou shall renew the face of the earth.

Let us pray. O God, Who, by the light of the Holy Spirit didst instruct the heart of the faithful. Grant that by the same Spirit, we may be truly wise and ever rejoice in His holy consolation. Through Christ our Lord. Amen.

Creed. Our Father. Hail Mary (3×).
Glory be.

O my Jesus, forgive us our sins, save us from the fires of hell, lead all souls to Heaven, especially those who are most in need of your mercy.

FIRST SORROWFUL MYSTERY
The Agony in the Garden

Petition. May the Lord grant us the grace of perfect sorrow for our sins and a perfect obedience to His holy will. Amen.

Consolation. Dearest Agonizing Jesus, we console Thee for the sweat of Blood Thou did shed in the garden of Gethsemane during Thy sorrowful agony.

Reparation. We make reparation for the crime of abortion of unborn babies, which is now regarded as a right for women.

Atonement Prayer. For Your Precious Blood shed for mankind, we are sorry for all the sins committed against Thee O Lord. St. Michael the Archangel with your light enlighten us, with your wings protect us, and with your sword defend us. Amen.

Our Father. Hail Mary (10×).
Glory be. O my Jesus.

SECOND SORROWFUL MYSTERY
The Scourging at the Pillar

Petition. May the Lord grant us the grace to mortify our senses perfectly. Amen.

Consolation. Dearest Agonizing Jesus Christ, we console Thee for the torrent of Blood You shed during Thy scourging at the pillar.

Reparation. We make reparation for the blood of innocent people who are tortured to death daily in various parts of the world.

Atonement Prayer. For Thy Precious Blood shed for mankind, we are sorry for all the sins committed against Thee O Lord. St. Michael the Archangel with your light enlighten us, with your wings protect us, and with your sword defend us. Amen.

Our Father. Hail Mary (10×).
Glory be. O my Jesus.

THIRD SORROWFUL MYSTERY
The Crowning with Thorns

Petition. May the Lord grant us the grace of true contempt for the world, its honors and riches. Amen.

Consolation. Dearest Agonizing Jesus Christ, we console Thee for the Blood which flowed from Thy Sacred Head during Thy painful crowning with Thorns.

Reparation. We make reparation for the crime of innocent people who are abducted and killed in cold blood.

Atonement Prayer. For Thy Precious Blood shed for mankind, we are sorry for all the sins committed against Thee O Lord. St. Michael the Archangel with your light enlighten us, with your wings protect us, and with your sword defend us. Amen.

Our Father. Hail Mary (10×).
Glory be. O my Jesus

FOURTH SORROWFUL MYSTERY
The Carrying of the Cross

Petition. May the Lord grant us the grace of patiently carrying our crosses everyday of our lives, in imitation of His footsteps. Amen.

Consolation. Dearest Agonizing Jesus Christ, we console Thee for the blood Thou did shed on the streets of Jerusalem on the way to Calvary.

Reparation. We make reparation for the innocent people who are killed during protests against oppression and suppression by evil rulers, and for women who are abused and murdered.

Atonement Prayer. For Thy Precious Blood shed for mankind, we are sorry for all the sins committed against Thee O Lord. St. Michael the Archangel with your light enlighten us, with your wings protect us, and with your sword defend us. Amen.

Our Father. Hail Mary (10x).
Glory be. O my Jesus.

FIFTH SORROWFUL MYSTERY
The Crucifixion & Death of Our Lord

Petition. May the Lord grant us the grace of horror for sin, love of the Cross and holy death for ourselves. May He be merciful to all those in their last agony. Amen.

Consolation. Dearest Agonizing Jesus Christ, we console Thee for the Blood Thou did shed from Thy Sacred Hands and Feet, and Thy sacred Side pierced with a lance.

Reparation. We make reparation for the blood of those killed for their Catholic belief and practices.

Atonement Prayer. For Thy Precious Blood shed for mankind, we are sorry for all the sins committed against Thee O Lord. St. Michael the Archangel with your light enlighten us, with your wings protect us, and with your sword defend us. Amen.

Our Father. Hail Mary (10×).
Glory be. O my Jesus.

CONCLUSION

Hail Holy Queen, Mother of mercy. Hail our life, our sweetness and our hope. To You do we cry, poor banished children of Eve. To You do we raise up heart mourning and weeping in this valley of tears. Turn then, most gracious advocate, Your eyes of mercy towards us. And after this our exile, show unto us the Blessed fruit of Your womb, Jesus. O Clement, O loving, O sweet Virgin Mary.

V. Pray for us O Holy Mother of God.
R. That we may be made worthy of the promises of Christ.

Let us pray. O God, whose only Begotten Son, by His life, death and resurrection, has purchased for us the reward of eternal life. Grant, we beseech Thee, that, meditating upon the mysteries of the most Holy Rosary of the Blessed Virgin Mary, we may imitate what they contain and obtain what they promise, through the same Christ our Lord.

V. Most Sacred Heart of Jesus.
R. Have mercy on us.
V. Immaculate of Mary.
R. Pray for us.
V. St. Joseph.
R. Pray for us.
V. St. John the Evangelist.
R. Pray for us.
V. St. Louis Maria de Montfort.
R. Pray for us.

PRAYER TO THE CRUCIFIED LORD JESUS CHRIST

O Jesus, Who by reason of Thy burning love for us has willed to be crucified and to shed Thy Most Precious Blood for the redemption and salvation of our souls, look down upon us here gathered together in remembrance of Thy Most Sorrowful Passion and Death, fully trusting in Thy mercy; cleanse us from sin by Thy grace, sanctify our toil, give unto us and unto all those who are dear to us our daily bread, sweeten our sufferings, bless our families, and to the nations so sorely afflicted, grant Thy peace, which is the only true peace, so that by obeying Thy Commandments we may come at last to the glory of Heaven. Amen.

Continue prayers from page 8, ***Cross of Grace****.*

SATURDAY

INTRODUCTION

General Intention. Consolation for the Sorrows of the Most Blessed Virgin Mary. Reparation for the blasphemies against the Blessed Mother of God.

Opening Hymn. God of Mercy. (*as on page 4, or any Lenten Hymn*)

Declaration of Intention. Dearest Agonizing Jesus Christ, I console Thee and adore Thy Most Precious Blood, in reparation for my sins and the sins of the whole world.

V. Come O Holy Ghost and fill the hearts of the faithful.
R. And enkindle in them the fire of Thy Love
V. Send forth Thy Spirit and they shall be created.
R. And Thou shall renew the face of the earth.

Let us pray. O God, Who, by the light of the Holy Ghost, didst instruct the heart of the faithful. Grant that by the same Spirit, we may be truly wise and ever rejoice in His holy consolation. Through Christ our Lord. Amen.

Creed. Our Father. Hail Mary (10×).
Glory be. O my Jesus.

O my Jesus, forgive us our sins, save us from the fires of hell, lead all souls to Heaven, especially those who are most in need of your mercy.

FIRST SORROWFUL MYSTERY
The Agony in the Garden

Petition. May the Lord grant us the grace of perfect sorrow for our sins and a perfect obedience to His holy will. Amen.

Consolation. Dearest Agonizing Jesus Christ, we console Thee for the anguish of Thy oly Mother during Your agony in the Garden, as we recall the sword of sorrow that pierced her heart at the prophecy of the holy Simeon during Thy presentation in the Temple.

Reparation. We make reparation for the acts of disdain for Thy Blessed Mother by those Catholics who do not acknowledge her dignity.

Atonement Prayer. Let us sing with You, Virgin Mother, and love with You your Son our Lord, Jesus Christ who died for us. St. Michael the Archangel with your light enlighten us, with your wings protect us, and with your sword defend us. Amen.

Our Father. Hail Mary (10×).
Glory be. O my Jesus.

SECOND SORROWFUL MYSTERY
The Scourging at the Pillar

Petition. May the Lord grant us the grace to mortify our senses perfectly. Amen.

Consolation. Dearest Lord Jesus Christ, we console Thee for the anguish of Thy most Holy Mother watching Thee being scourged at the pillar, as we recall the sword of sorrow that pierced her heart when she lost Thee for three days in the Temple.

Reparation. We make reparation for the sins of Christians who pretend to worship Thee, but blaspheme and insult Thy most Holy Mother.

Atonement Prayer. Let us sing with You, Virgin Mother, and love with You your Son our Lord, Jesus Christ who died for us. St. Michael the Archangel with your light enlighten us, with your wings protect us, and with your sword defend us. Amen.

Our Father. Hail Mary (10×).
Glory be. O my Jesus.

THIRD SORROWFUL MYSTERY
The Crowning with Thorns

Petition. May the Lord grant us the grace of true contempt for the world, its honors and riches. Amen.

Consolation. Dearest agonizing Jesus Christ, we console Thee for the anguish of Thy most Holy Mother during Thy crowning with thorns, as we recall the sword of sorrow that pierced her heart during the flight into Egypt.

Reparation. We make reparation for the crime of those who desecrate and despoil images of Thy Blessed Mother out of hatred and contempt for her.

Atonement Prayer. Let us sing with You, Virgin Mother, and love with You your Son our Lord, Jesus Christ who died for us. St. Michael the Archangel with your light enlighten us, with your wings protect us, and with your sword defend us. Amen.

Our Father. Hail Mary (10×).
Glory be. O my Jesus.

FOURTH SORROWFUL MYSTERY
The Carrying of the Cross

Petition. May the Lord grant us the grace of patiently carrying our crosses everyday of our lives, in imitation of His footsteps. Amen.

Consolation. Dearest Agonizing Jesus Christ, we console Thee for the anguish of Thy most Holy Mother when she met Thee on the way to Calvary, and the sword of sorrow that pierced her heart.

Reparation. We make reparation for those Catholics who left the Church in search of miracles in other religious sects, where they participate in acts of desrespect and blasphemy against Thy most Holy Mother.

Atonement Prayer. Let us sing with you, Virgin Mother, and love with you your Son our Lord, Jesus Christ who died for us. St. Michael the Archangel with your light enlighten us, with your wings protect us, and with your sword defend us. Amen.

Our Father. Hail Mary (10×).
Glory be. O my Jesus.

FIFTH SORROWFUL MYSTERY
The Crucifixion & Death of Our Lord

Petition. May the Lord grant us the grace of horror for sin, love of the Cross and holy death for ourselves. May He be merciful to all those in their last agony. Amen.

Consolation. Dearest Agonizing Jesus Christ, we console Thee for the sword of sorrow that pierced the Heart of Thy most Holy Mother, multiple times at the foot of the Cross; from the time You were nailed to It, until Thy death and burial.

Reparation. We make reparation for the acts of disrespect towards the images of the Blessed Mother that were removed from Your churches out of contempt, and disregard of her genuine messages to the Church and the world.

Atonement Prayer. Let us sing with you, Virgin Mother, and love with you your Son our Lord, Jesus Christ who died for us. St. Michael the Archangel with your light enlighten us, with your wings protect us, and with your sword defend us. Amen.

Our Father. Hail Mary (10×).
Glory be. O my Jesus.

CONCLUSION

Hail Holy Queen, Mother of mercy. Hail our life, our sweetness and our hope. To You do cry, poor banished children of Eve. To You do we raise up heart mourning and weeping in this valley of tears. Turn then, most gracious advocate, your eyes of mercy towards us. And after this our exile, show unto us the Blessed fruit of your womb, Jesus. O Clement, O loving, O sweet Virgin Mary.

V. Pray for us O Holy Mother of God.
R. That we may be made worthy of the promises of Christ.

Let us pray. O God, whose only Begotten Son, by His life, death and resurrection, has purchased for us the reward of eternal life. Grant, we beseech Thee, that, meditating upon the mysteries of the most Holy Rosary of the Blessed Virgin Mary, we may imitate what they contain and obtain what they promise, through the same Christ our Lord.

V. Most Sacred Heart of Jesus.
R. Have mercy on us.
V. Immaculate of Mary.
R. Pray for us.
V. St. Joseph.
R. Pray for us.
V. St. John the Evangelist.
R. Pray for us.
V. St. Louis Maria de Montfort.
R. Pray for us.

AN ACT OF REPARATION FOR BLASPHEMIES AGAINST THE BLESSED VIRGIN MARY

Most glorious Virgin Mary, Mother of God and our Mother, turn thine eyes of pity upon us, miserable sinners; we are sore afflicted by the many evils that surround us in this life, but especially do we feel our hearts break within us upon hearing the dreadful insults and blasphemies uttered against thee, O Virgin Immaculate. O how these impious sayings offend the infinite Majesty of God and His Only-Begotten Son, Jesus Christ! How they provoke His indignation and give us cause to fear the terrible effects of His vengeance! Would that the sacrifice of our lives might avail to put an end to such outrages and blasphemies; were it so, how gladly we would make it, for we desire, O most holy Mother, to love You and to honor You with all our hearts, since this is the will of God. And just because we love You, we will do all that is in our power to make You honored and loved by all men. In the meantime, do thou, our merciful Mother, the supreme comforter of the afflicted, accept this act of reparation which we offer thee for ourselves and for all our families, as well as for all who impiously blaspheme thee, not knowing what they say. Do thou obtain for them from Almighty God the grace of conversion, and thus render more manifest and more glorious Your kindness, Your power and thy great mercy. May they join with us in proclaiming You blessed among women, the Immaculate Virgin and most compassionate Mother of God. Amen.

Hail Mary (3x).

PRAYER TO OUR LADY OF SORROWS

O Mother of sorrow, by the anguish and love by which thou didst stand at the foot of the Cross, stand by me too in my last agony. To thy maternal heart, I commend the last three hours of my life. Offer these hours to the Eternal Father in union with the agony of thy sorrowful heart; in atonement for my sins. Offer to the Eternal Father, the Most Precious Blood of thy Son mingled with thy tears on calvary, that I may obtain the grace of receiving Holy Communion with the most fervent love and contrition before my death; that I may breathe forth my soul in the adorable presence of Jesus. Dearest Mother, when the moment of my death hath at late come, present me as your child to Jesus. Ask Him to forgive me having offended Him, for I know not what I did. Beg Him to receive me into His Kingdom of glory, to be united with Him forever. Amen.

Continue prayers from page 8, ***Cross of Grace.***

Fr. Evaristus Eshiowu, is a retired priest of the Priestly Fraternity of St. Peter (FSSP), in residence at the FSSP parish in the Catholic Diocese of Sacramento, California, USA.

www.ingramcontent.com/pod-product-compliance
Lightning Source LLC
LaVergne TN
LVHW061047070526
838201LV00074B/5209